All the material in this book was confirmed as accurate at the time of publication.

The names, trademarks, and logos of the named entities and brands profiled in this book are the property of their respective owners and are used solely for identification purposes. This book is a publication of Quarto Publishing plc and it has not been prepared, approved, endorsed, or licensed by any other brand, person, or entity.

For Murray, who always brings the sunshine.—H.A.

To my friends, Josh and Rachel Covarrubias.—J.M-P.

Text © 2024 Heather Alexander L.L.C. Illustrations © 2024 J. Moffat-Peña

First published in 2024 by Wide Eyed Editions, an imprint of The Quarto Group.
100 Cummings Center, Suite 265D, Beverly, MA 01915, USA.
T +1 978-282-9590 www.Quarto.com

A CIP record for this book is available from the Library of Congress.

ISBN 978-0-7112-8145-5
eBook ISBN 978-0-7112-8146-2

The illustrations were created digitally
Set in Quicksand and Thirsty Script

Designer: Myrto Dimitrakoulia
Editor: Corinne Lucas
Production Controller: Dawn Cameron
Art Director: Karissa Santos
Publisher: Debbie Foy

Manufactured in Guangdong, China TT122023

9 8 7 6 5 4 3 2 1

Only in FLORIDA

Written by **Heather Alexander** · Illustrated by **J. Moffat–Peña**

WIDE EYED EDITIONS

Contents

N

W · E

S

PENSACOLA

GULF OF
MEXICO

Let's meet in the middle!
The state's GEOGRAPHIC
CENTER—an imaginary
point—is believed to be
12 miles north-northwest
of Brooksville.

Welcome to Florida

Have you ever dreamed of diving for pirate treasure, winning a sandcastle competition, riding a swamp buggy, swimming with manatees, staying at an underwater hotel, and visiting a fairy-tale castle? Then let's hop into our (imaginary) sunny yellow convertible (top down, of course!) and take a wacky road trip up and down the long and narrow Sunshine State. Be sure to wear your bathing suit (and sunscreen!), because in Florida, we're never more than 60 miles from the ocean. With the warm rays and warm water, it often feels like it's summer forever. As we travel from coast to coast to coast (there are lots of different coasts!), we'll keep an eye out for the many offbeat, amazing, and just plain weird history, buildings, attractions, festivals, plants, animals, and people that make Florida phenomenal, fantastic, and definitely one of a kind.

Florida is the only state
that borders the GULF
OF MEXICO and the
ATLANTIC OCEAN.

JACKSONVILLE

TALLAHASSEE

ATLANTIC OCEAN

PANAMA CITY

GAINESVILLE

It's easy to get wet! Florida has more than 8,000 LAKES AND PONDS!

CAPE CANAVERAL

ORLANDO

TAMPA

FORT LAUDERDALE

NAPLES

MIAMI

Just add water! Florida is a PENINSULA, which means it is surrounded by water on three sides.

EVERGLADES NATIONAL PARK

THE KEYS

STRAITS OF FLORIDA

10

Jacksonville is the LARGEST CITY by area (875 square miles) in the contiguous U.S.—that's the lower 48 states. (Four Alaskan cities are larger!)

Soul music legend RAY CHARLES learned to play piano at the school for deaf and blind students in St. Augustine (he was blind but not deaf).

In 1900, Jacksonville brothers James Weldon Johnson and John Rosamond Johnson wrote "LIFT EVERY VOICE AND SING," now known as the "Black National Anthem."

The enormous, rainbow-light FRIENDSHIP FOUNTAIN in downtown Jax blasts streams of water super high into the air.

It makes perfect sense that such a large city has the country's LARGEST URBAN PARK SYSTEM with over 80,000 acres of parks, nature preserves, athletic fields, playgrounds, and even dog parks!

Boo! Is ST. AUGUSTINE LIGHTHOUSE, with its black-and-white spiral and red top, haunted? Some people think so. But that doesn't stop visitors from climbing the 219 steps to the observation deck!

You can do the backstroke while watching football! There are two SWIMMING POOLS inside EverBank Field, the stadium where the Jacksonville Jaguars play.

Floridians William Fadeley Jr. and Eugene Hajtovik set the world record for LONGEST JOURNEY ON AN AIRBOAT. In 1986, they traveled 1,100 miles along the Intracoastal Waterway from Jacksonville to New York City (NYC) in 13 days.

Jacksonville, or "JAX", was named for General Andrew Jackson, the first military governor of Florida (and later the nation's seventh president). Weirdly, Jackson never visited Jacksonville.

Dating back to the 1970s, Kona Skatepark in Jacksonville is the nation's oldest operating, privately owned OUTDOOR SKATEPARK.

Nana, the tallest sand dune (about 60 feet) in Florida, can be found on Amelia Island's American Beach. This beach was founded in 1935 by Florida's first Black millionaire, A. L. LEWIS. It was one of the few beaches to welcome Black families throughout segregation.

CASTILLO DE SAN MARCOS in St. Augustine is the nation's oldest masonry (stone) fort. Starting in 1672, the Spanish built the fort to defend the city from pirates and the British, and wow, did it work! Cannonballs bounced off the crushed coquina (seashell) walls instead of shattering them!

First Coast

First things first . . . let's begin at the beginning! We're starting our journey in Northeast Florida, otherwise known as the "First Coast." The nickname comes from St. Augustine, the nation's oldest permanent European settlement. It's also the first section of coast you reach if you enter Florida from the state of Georgia. Here you'll find tons of historical landmarks that'll pull you back in time alongside the excitement of sprawling, modern Jacksonville. Plus, because it's fun-in-the-sun Florida, there's plenty of glistening sand and welcoming waves. Race you to the ocean . . . who's going to be the first one in?

Stats & Facts

FAST FACTS

ABBREVIATION: FL
CAPITAL: Tallahassee
STATEHOOD: March 3, 1845, 27th state
NUMBER OF COUNTIES: 67
POPULATION: 22+ million, making it the third most populous state, after California and Texas.
AREA: 65,758 square miles, making it the 22nd largest state.

STATE SUPERLATIVES

- Florida is the FLATTEST STATE in the nation. Its highest natural point, Britton Hill (345 feet above sea level), is the lowest high point of any state.
- Florida is the HOTTEST state, with an average temperature of 72 degrees Fahrenheit. It's also the MOST HUMID state.
- Florida has the MOST THUNDERSTORMS and LIGHTNING.
- Florida has the SECOND LONGEST SHORELINE (after Alaska), measuring 8,436 miles.
- Florida has more GOLF COURSES than any other state—over 1,250!
- Florida has hosted the most NFL SUPER BOWLS—17 (and counting)!
- Tampa's Bayshore Boulevard is the world's LONGEST CONTINUOUS SIDEWALK.
- Florida has the most species of CARNIVOROUS PLANTS of any state.
- Everglades National Park is the nation's LARGEST SUBTROPICAL WILDERNESS.
- Florida has the world's MOST UNDERWATER SPRINGS—more than 700!
- One of the world's two NATURALLY ROUND LAKES is at DeFuniak Springs.

The official STATE FLAG has the state seal in the center of a red X (called a saltire) on a white background. Up until 1900, the flag had only the seal. It's believed the saltire was added so the flag wouldn't be mistaken for a white surrender flag.

Next-Door Neighbors

NORTH: Georgia, Alabama   **WEST:** Alabama,

IN THE NATION, FLORIDA PRODUCES THE MOST:

- Bell peppers
- Cucumbers
- Grapefruit
- Oranges
- Snap peas
- Sugarcane
- Watermelons

In 1985, the STATE SEAL got a redo to fix the many mistakes. The Indigenous woman from the Western Plains was replaced with a Seminole woman from Florida. The cocoa palm was changed to the sabal palm that grows in Florida. And the background mountains were tossed out because, hello, Florida is *really* flat!

Florida's nickname, the "SUNSHINE STATE", isn't exactly accurate. Florida has an average of 237 days of sunshine per year, but other states get *way* more rays, including Arizona, Nevada, and New Mexico.

It's believed the name FLORIDA came from Spanish explorer Juan Ponce de León. He was probably honoring Spain's Easter celebration Pascua Florida, or "Feast of Flowers," since that's when he landed on the peninsula. Mark your calendar: Pascua Florida Day is on April 2 every year.

Gulf of Mexico   SOUTH: Straits of Florida   EAST: Atlantic Ocean

Space Coast

Do you want a front-row seat to the future? The heart of the U.S. space program is found on Florida's "Space Coast." NASA (National Aeronautics and Space Administration), along with companies such as SpaceX and Blue Origin, launch and test a lot of their rockets at Cape Canaveral Space Force Station and John F. Kennedy Space Center. Did you know the Space Coast is the only place in the world where you can go boogie boarding in the afternoon then watch a rocket blast to the stars in the evening? The countdown to an out-of-this-world adventure has begun!

The Vehicle Assembly Building (VAB)—where rockets and spaceships are put together—is the LARGEST ONE-STORY BUILDING in the world. It's about the size of six football fields! Its entry bays have the world's largest doors, which take almost an hour to fully open or close. Its ceiling is so high (525 feet) that rain clouds can form inside!

Since 1968, all ASTRONAUT-CONTROLLED SPACEFLIGHTS have launched from the Kennedy Space Center on Merritt Island. Cape Canaveral is separated from Merritt Island by the Banana River, named because wild bananas once grew on its banks.

Brevard County's 321 AREA CODE is taken from the 3 . . . 2 . . . 1 . . . launch countdown!

NASA chose Cape Canaveral as its launchpad because the land juts out into the Atlantic Ocean, allowing any falling rocket debris to plop into the water instead of a populated area.

We're going back to the Moon (people haven't visited since 1972). The ARTEMIS PROGRAM hopes to set up a permanent base camp on the Moon and eventually fly to Mars.

The Eagle has landed! On July 16, 1969, Neil Armstrong, Buzz Aldrin, and Michael Collins blasted off from the Kennedy Space Center inside the Apollo 11 capsule on the Saturn V rocket. Four days later, Armstrong and Aldrin became the first people to LAND ON THE MOON.

SPACE SHUTTLE ATLANTIS is displayed at Kennedy Space Center at a 43.21-degree angle (think: 4, 3, 2, 1 . . . blastoff!).

Do you have what it takes to explore Mars? Test your intergalactic skills at the ASTRONAUT TRAINING EXPERIENCE (ATX). There's a microgravity chair and a simulated spacewalk.

Weather forecasting got a whole lot easier after TIROS-1, the world's FIRST WEATHER SATELLITE, was launched into orbit from Cape Canaveral in 1960. It let meteorologists see clouds over faraway oceans and helped to predict hurricanes.

FLORIDA SCRUB JAYS live solely in the Sunshine State, and there's only about 4,000 left in the world. They hop along the ground, searching for acorns to eat now and bury for a snack later. Look for them at Scrub-Jay Trail at Merritt Island.

The Space Coast is also home to Cocoa Beach, the surfing capital of the eastern U.S. Here you'll find Ron Jon Surf Shop, the world's LARGEST SURF SHOP.

The lagoon water at Merritt Island National Wildlife Refuge in Titusville glows bright blue-green from the light of BIOLUMINESCENT COMB JELLYFISH. Talk about out of this world!

It's super weird that MOONSTONE is the state gem. It's not found naturally in Florida or even on the Moon. Why was it chosen? To commemorate the 1969 Moon landing.

History Timeline

Over 12,000 years ago The first people arrive to live in what is now known as Florida.

By the 1500s More than a dozen different Indigenous tribes live in what is today called Florida, including the Ais, Apalachee, Calusa, Jaega, Tequesta, and Timucua.

1513 Juan Ponce de León is believed to be the first European to land in Florida. He is searching for gold and territory for Spain. He goes home but returns in 1531. The Calusa people shoot him with a fatal poison arrow.

1845 Florida becomes the 27th state. The first state flag bears the slogan "Let us alone."

1835–42 The Second Seminole War (there ends up being three wars!) erupts when the U.S. tries to force the Seminoles to move west. The long war costs the Seminoles their homeland. A few hundred escape to the Everglades.

1821 Spain trades Florida *again*—this time to the U.S. for Spanish rule over Texas.

1861 The Civil War starts. Florida joins the Confederacy.

1883 Henry Flagler builds a railroad along the state's Atlantic Coast, while Henry Plant builds one along the Gulf Coast. Wetlands are drained and hotels are built.

1895 During the Great Freeze, much of Central Florida's citrus crop is destroyed. Many growers move elsewhere. It takes decades for the citrus industry to blossom again.

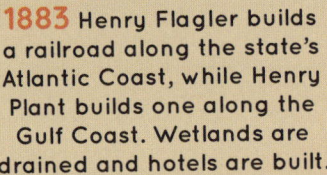

1989 Miami resident Ileana Ros-Lehtinen becomes the first Hispanic woman and the first Cuban American elected to the U.S. Congress.

1971 Walt Disney World opens near Orlando, once an area of citrus groves and cattle ranches.

1968 The nation's first clown college is founded in Venice. Auditions include juggling and throwing pies!

1993 Miami-born Janet Reno is named the first female U.S. Attorney General.

2004 Four hurricanes pummel the state in just six weeks!

2005 Winter Park resident Mel (Melquiades Rafael) Martinez is the first Cuban American elected to the U.S. Senate.

1559 Spanish conquistador Don Tristan de Luna sails into what is now Pensacola Bay with 1,500 colonists. They soon lose their supplies to a hurricane, get sick, and leave.

1564 French Huguenots build Fort Caroline at what is now Jacksonville, but the Spanish destroy it so the French leave too.

1565 St. Augustine, the oldest permanent European settlement in North America, is founded by Spain's Pedro Menéndez de Avilés. A lot of Native Americans are tragically killed.

1700s The Seminole Nation is formed when tribes from Florida, Georgia, and Alabama come together to defend their way of life. Later in the century, they're joined by enslaved Africans and Black Americans who fled plantations.

1783 As part of the peace treaty, which ends the Revolutionary War, Spain takes Florida back from Britain.

1763 Spain trades with Britain. They swap what's now Florida for what's now Havana, Cuba.

1738 Fort Mose, north of St. Augustine, becomes the first free Black town and has its own militia. It only lasts a few decades.

1903 President Theodore Roosevelt establishes the first national wildlife refuge at Pelican Island to protect brown pelicans from being hunted for their feathers.

1914 The world's first scheduled passenger airline flies from St. Petersburg to Tampa. Tickets are $5.

1947 Everglades National Park is established.

1961 Astronaut Alan Shepard blasts off from Cape Canaveral Space Center (later Kennedy Space Center), becoming the first American in space.

1959–1973 After Communists take over Cuba, more than 200,000 Cubans settle in South Florida.

1956 The Tallahassee Bus Boycott is one of the nation's first public Civil Rights Movement protests against racial segregation on buses and public beaches, and in stores and schools.

2010 Tar washes up on Panhandle beaches from an enormous offshore oil spill three states away in the Gulf of Mexico, and harms wildlife.

2017 Stephanie Murphy is the first Vietnamese American woman elected to the U.S. Congress.

2022 Orion spacecraft, the first step in NASA's Artemis Moon to Mars exploration mission, launches from Cape Canaveral.

Author Marjorie Kinnan Rawlings wrote *The Yearling* at her cottage in wooded CROSS CREEK.

Keep your eyes peeled for the farming town of LaCrosse, known as the "POTATO DISTRICT" of Florida.

On the University of Florida campus, over 450,000 bats hang out in the world's LARGEST OCCUPIED BAT HOUSES. Just after sunset, they fly out in a *whoosh* in search of dinner. The bats can eat more than two tons of insects a night!

A cut above! The FLORIDA FOREST FESTIVAL in Perry celebrates all the people who work in and protect the forests. Their chainsaw and crosscut competitions are the best you ever *saw*!

North Central Florida

Hop into the saddle to go horsin' around the rolling green pastures of North Central Florida. We'll canter first to Ocala, famous for its champion thoroughbred horse farms, then gallop north to Gainesville, home of the University of Florida. After a dip in a refreshing spring-fed lake, we'll ride west to the Big Bend region (the spot where the state begins to curve) and swap our steed for a canoe to paddle down a sun-drenched, oak-lined river. We're not *foaling* around—the center of Florida is where the action is!

Florida waters are home to more than 40 shark species. While it's incredibly rare for them to bother humans, the Florida Museum in Gainesville is home to the INTERNATIONAL SHARK ATTACK FILE (ISAF), the world's only scientifically documented database of all known shark attacks.

Do you know the names of the University of Florida Gators' TWO REPTILIAN MASCOTS? Albert and Alberta!

Ocala National Forest is the southernmost forest in the continental U.S. and has the world's LARGEST SAND PINES FOREST.

Many FAMOUS RACEHORSES were trained or bred in Marion County, including Needles (named because of his many trips to the vet), who was the first Florida-raised horse to win the Kentucky Derby.

Floyd "Sonny" Tillman and his wife Lucille's slow-smoked barbecue restaurant chain, SONNY'S BBQ, started in Gainesville in 1968. Fun fact: the company employs a Chief Kindness Officer, who finds ways for staff and customers to spread kindness.

With over 2,000 HORSE FARMS, Marion County has more horses than any other county in the U.S. and gave Ocala the nickname "Horse Capital of the World."

Animals crossing ahead! The LAND BRIDGE near Ocala was the first in the country. It allows wildlife and pedestrians to safely cross the busy highway.

Butterfly magic! Hundreds of exotic butterflies flutter about—and on you—at the Florida Museum of Natural History's Butterfly Rainforest in Gainesville. The McGuire Center for Lepidoptera and Biodiversity at the University of Florida boasts the WORLD'S LARGEST BUTTERFLY COLLECTION—over 12 million!

Spectacular Sports

Sunny skies, green fields, fast speedways, and warm waves and wakes make Florida one of the nation's top spots for sports!

Can you name all 12 professional SUNSHINE STATE SPORTS TEAMS? (See the last page in this book for the list.)

Wellington is all about horses and POLO. Polo is the fast, hoof-pounding sport played on horseback. Riders use mallets to hit a ball into a goal.

With more GOLF COURSES than any other state, it's no wonder that Florida is home to the World Golf Hall of Fame and Museum. Head to St. Augustine to tee off.

In 1972, the MIAMI DOLPHINS became the only team to play a perfect season, finishing the season 17–0.

Hialeah Park Race Track was the first major racetrack where a FEMALE JOCKEY—Diane Crump in 1969—was allowed to compete.

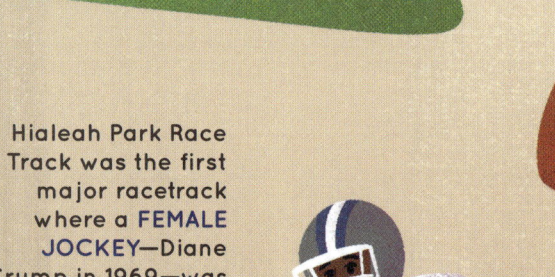

Jacksonville native ROBERT "BULLET BOB" HAYES is the only person to win both an Olympic gold medal (he won two in 1964: men's 100-meter dash and 4 × 100-meter relay) and a Super Bowl ring.

Called the world's LONGEST RIVER SAILBOAT RACE, the annual Mug Race stretches for 38 nautical miles between Palatka and Orange Park on the St. Johns River.

EMMITT SMITH, born and raised in Pensacola, holds the NFL's career rushing record—18,355 yards!

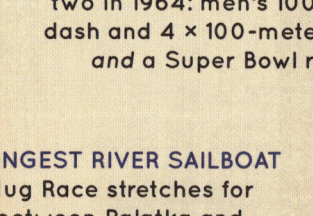

In Miami Beach in 1964, young CASSIUS CLAY (who later became Muhammad Ali) beat reigning champ Sonny Liston in less than 20 minutes in his first world heavyweight boxing championship fight.

Sun's out, batters up! Every winter, 15 Major League Baseball (MLB) teams travel to Florida for SPRING TRAINING. The teams that train in the Sunshine State are called the "Grapefruit League," while the other 15 teams who head to Arizona are the "Cactus League."

In 2020, Miami Marlins' Kim Ng became the FIRST FEMALE MLB GENERAL MANAGER.

Babe Ruth hit his LONGEST HOME RUN ever recorded—587 feet—during a spring-training game in Tampa in 1919.

JAI ALAI, a handball sport from Spain, was once very popular in South Florida. The ball, or pelota, is one of the hardest and fastest in sports, and players try to catch it in a basket-like cesta.

Start your engines! The famous DAYTONA 500 is a 200-lap race around Daytona International Speedway's oval track. Stock cars need major speed in order to bank the very high, steep curves.

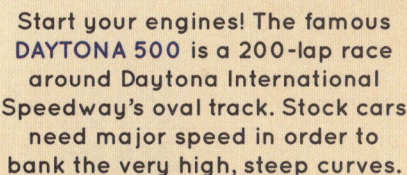

CHAMPION

Although South Florida tennis champs COCO GAUFF (winner of the 2023 U.S. Open at age 19) and SLOANE STEPHENS are rivals on the court, they never let that ruin their friendship.

The ORANGE BOWL was first played in Miami in 1935. Do you know what's piled inside the trophy that goes to the winning college football team? Actual oranges!

In 1990, the first official WAKEBOARDING competition took place in Orlando, and a decade or so later wakeskating took off. A wakeskating rider is not attached to the board, allowing them to do many of the same tricks as a skateboarder . . . but on the water.

Kelly Slater, a record-breaking 11-time world champion, started SURFING at age five on a bodyboard in his hometown of Cocoa Beach.

In 1984, Orlando resident and Air Force command pilot Joe Kittinger was the first person to fly a gas HOT-AIR BALLOON across the Atlantic Ocean alone.

What a view! The Wheel at ICON park Orlando is the SECOND TALLEST OBSERVATIONAL WHEEL in the U.S. (400 feet). And it's fitted with 64,000 dazzling color-changing lights!

In 2014, the world's largest gathering of fans dressed as TEENAGE MUTANT NINJA TURTLES (1,394!) happened at Orlando's Nickelodeon Suites Resort.

Orlando is in Orange County, named after the many citrus groves that used to be in the area. But it was originally called MOSQUITO COUNTY!

Stomach flip! SeaWorld Orlando's Ice Breaker ROLLER COASTER has four airtime-filled launches that go backward and forward.

Walt Disney World's SPACE MOUNTAIN was the first indoor roller coaster where riders were in total darkness for the whole ride.

Orlando has over a hundred lakes, many formed by GIANT SINKHOLES.

So cool! DOLE WHIP, a pineapple-flavored frozen treat, and CITRUS SWIRL soft serve are delicious Disney desserts.

Orlando

Make sure you're strapped in, because we're going for a whirl and a twirl in Orlando, the country's amusement park capital. This fun city, located right in the middle of the state, is home to Walt Disney World, Universal Studios, SeaWorld, Legoland, and so many other theme parks. Here in the "City Beautiful," you'll find roller coasters, water slides, lazy rivers, spinning teacups, princesses and wizards, and mind-blowing attractions galore. Let's get in line!

Six species of sharks swim inches away as you glide on a moving sidewalk through one of the LONGEST UNDERWATER VIEWING TUNNELS at SeaWorld Orlando.

Orlando is home to the WORLD'S LARGEST ENTERTAINMENT MCDONALD'S, known as "Epic McD," which boasts over a hundred arcade games and an oversized menu that includes pizza and waffles!

Catch the Hogwarts Express train from PLATFORM 9 ¾ at Universal Studios' Wizarding World of Harry Potter!

More than 200 pairs of SUNGLASSES are handed in to Walt Disney World's lost and found every day. That's over 73,000 a year!

More than 50 SWANS of five different species live in Lake Eola.

Trees & Flowers

Here's a riddle: what kind of Florida tree can you hold in your hand? A *palm* tree! Florida's climate and soil helps plants grow and grow and grow—with magnolia and dogwood trees in the north, mangrove forests and bald cypress in the swamps, tall saw grass in the marshes, and sea grapes on the dunes. Time to take a tour!

Orange you glad the state flower is the sweet-smelling ORANGE BLOSSOM? The first orange seeds were brought to Florida by the Spanish. June 27 is National Orange Blossom Day.

Pierson is called the "FERN CAPITAL OF THE WORLD." The town's ferneries (a fancy name for fern farms) supply most of the fern fronds used in floral arrangements in the U.S.

Double and triple ouch! The spiky SANDSPUR is a nasty weed that attacks! Stepping on a thorny burr with your bare foot is sure to bring prickly pain.

About 95 percent of all CALADIUMS are grown in Lake Placid, the "Caladium Capital of the World" and home to the annual Caladium Festival.

The colorful, daisy-like COREOPSIS is the state wildflower. Its other name is "tickseed" because its tiny seeds look like parasitic ticks!

Native to South Florida, the GUMBO LIMBO TREE's nickname is "tourist tree," because its peeling red bark looks like the skin of a sunburned tourist!

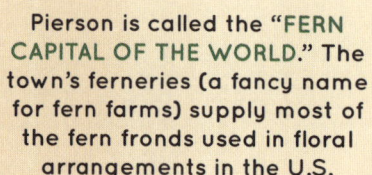

Ouch! SAW GRASS, found in marshes and swamps, has sharp teeth along the edges of its blades that can slice through clothing! Alligators and muskrats often use saw grass to build their nests.

Grapefruit got its name because it grows in clusters, like grapes do. Grapefruit were brought from the Caribbean in the 1800s and planted near Tampa. In the early 1900s, the FIRST PINK GRAPEFRUIT was discovered growing among yellow grapefruit in an orchard near Ellenton.

The rare and endangered TITUSVILLE MINT is endemic to Titusville, which means it grows nowhere else in the world!

An enormous BANYAN TREE (its canopy takes up roughly the size of a football field!) grows at the Edison and Ford Winter Estates in Fort Myers. It's believed to have been planted around 1925 when it was only 4 feet tall.

Purplicious! The native BEAUTYBERRY grows in clusters on shrubs along roadways and in forests. The berries taste bitter raw but can be cooked into a yummy jelly or a purple sauce to pour over ice cream.

The beautiful flowers of the HIBISCUS last for only one day!

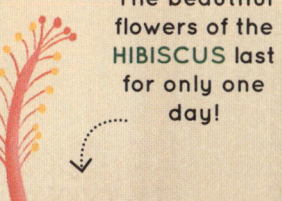

The state tree is the SABAL PALM, also known as the "palmetto." They're also called swamp cabbages, and if you've ever eaten a heart of palm, it comes from the sabal palm's core. Check out the Swamp Cabbage Festival in LaBelle!

SEA GRAPES taste like grapes but aren't true grapes. They're part of the buckwheat family, just like rhubarb. The plant helps keep sand dunes from eroding and protects sea turtles by blocking artificial light from their nests on beaches.

Want to see a nifty trick? The RESURRECTION FERN rises from the dead! During dry seasons, it "dies," turning brown and shriveling up. When it rains, the small fern springs quickly back to life, turning bright green and opening its fronds.

The Indian River is not technically a river. Two miles wide and 155 miles long, it is a TIDAL LAGOON and an estuary with brackish (slightly salty) water.

Indian River Lagoon is the MOST BIOLOGICALLY DIVERSE ESTUARY in the nation with over 4,000 species of plants and animals.

South Hutchinson Island is one o the few places in Florida you car RIDE A HORSE ON THE BEACH

The town of Wabasso was named after the town Ossabaw in Georgia—but SPELLED BACKWARD! What would your town's name spelled backward be?

The non-venomous ATLANTIC SALT MARSH SNAKE is only found in the Indian River Lagoon. About two feet long, they hide in burrows made by fiddler crabs or muskrats.

"The only easy day was yesterday!" is the motto of the U.S. Navy Seals. At the NATIONAL NAVY SEAL MUSEUM in Fort Pierce, meet the elite special forces who courageously jump from helicopters into enemy territory and even swim out of torpedo tubes on submarines.

SPRUCE BLUFF MOUND in the wetlands of Port St. Lucie was probably built by the Ais people about 2,000 years ago! The ceremonial or burial mound is around 18 feet tall.

At BLOWING ROCKS PRESERVE on Jupiter Island, the crashing sea shoots plumes of water up to 50 feet into the sky through holes in the limestone rock.

Stuart is called the "SAILFISH CAPITAL OF THE WORLD." The sailfish is the fastest fish in the ocean, able to reach speeds of nearly 70 miles per hour while leaping out of the water.

Juicy INDIAN RIVER CITRUS has been famous for being some of the best-tasting oranges since the early 1800s.

In the ancient cypress trees surrounding Blue Cypress Lake, hundreds of OSPREYS build their nests. These raptors only eat live fish.

The PURPLE GALLINULE'S long yellow toes let it walk on floating lily pads! And when its mom or dad calls, this amazingly colored aquatic bird does a funny run across the pads to reach them.

In 2016, scientists from Florida Atlantic University discovered bones that are believed to be 13,000 to 14,000 years old and from an EXTINCT SPECIES OF BISON in Vero Beach.

Treasure Coast

Keep your eyes open as we cruise the "Treasure Coast" along the state's Atlantic shore—millions of dollars of gold coins and jewels may wash up onto the beach! Back in 1715, 11 Spanish ships sailing from Cuba to Florida were wrecked during a hurricane, and treasure tumbled onto the ocean floor. But that's not the only treasure to be found—there's also the natural beauty of the beach, the barrier islands, the inlets, and the wildlife. Oh, look! There are two loveable manatees gliding alongside our kayak in the Indian River. What gems!

Museums & Attractions

Florida's high-flying thrills, surprising exhibits, and unusual museums never fail to entertain and delight! Hold on tight for a weird and wild ride!

Discover the fantastical world of the Spanish artist who painted the famous melting clocks at the SALVADOR DALÍ MUSEUM in St. Petersburg. Do you know how the museum's architect tested the strength of the huge spiral staircase? He had two rugby teams dance on it—to disco music!

Ahoy there, matey! Raise the Jolly Roger at the ST. AUGUSTINE PIRATE AND TREASURE MUSEUM and view over 800 pirate artifacts from the 1600s through to the present day.

The Morikami Museum and Japanese Gardens in Delray Beach has an incredible BONSAI collection. Bonsai means "a tree in a tray." Bonsai is an ancient East Asian art where you trim and shape a tiny tree in a container to represent, but not copy, trees in nature.

CORAL CASTLE MUSEUM near Homestead was hand-carved out of more than 1,100 tons of coral rock by Ed Leedskalnin. He even created a 9-ton gate that opens with the touch of a finger!

Vroom! The DON GARLITS MUSEUM OF DRAG RACING in Ocala is named after the Tampa-born racing legend, who won 144 national and 17 world championship titles and clocked speeds over 323 miles per hour in his "Swamp Rat" cars.

In the 1950s and 1960s, galleries in segregated Florida wouldn't sell the work of Black artists, so a group of 26 talented and resourceful Black artists sold their colorful Florida landscapes door-to-door or along roadsides. They became known as the FLORIDA HIGHWAYMEN. Today their artwork is displayed in the A. E. Backus Museum and Gallery in Fort Pierce and the Museum of Florida History in Tallahassee.

AMERICAN POLICE HALL OF FAME AND MUSEUM in Titusville is the nation's first law enforcement museum and features a Memorial Wall of over 9,000 officers who have lost their lives in service.

Trash talk! The country's only **GARBAGE TRUCK MUSEUM** in Sanford is loads of grimy fun.

Scream time! Iron Gwazi at Busch Gardens Tampa Bay, plunges riders down a 91-degree drop at 76 miles per hour! As of 2023, it was the tallest hybrid coaster (made from both wood and steel) in North America, and the **FASTEST AND STEEPEST HYBRID COASTER** in the world.

Take a twirl on the 155-foot-tall Midway Sky Eye, the nation's **LARGEST PORTABLE FERRIS WHEEL**, at the Florida State Fair in Tampa.

Climb through a real submarine and explore **SEALAB I**, the U.S. Navy's first underwater habitat, at the Man in the Sea Museum in Panama City Beach.

Lined with super fancy stores, WORTH AVENUE in Palm Beach is one of the nation's most luxurious shopping streets.

Former U.S. President Donald J. Trump made MAR-A-LAGO, his club in Palm Beach, his "winter White House" from 2016 to 2020.

In 1985, a hairdresser sunk his Rolls-Royce 85 feet underwater off Palm Beach to form an ARTIFICIAL REEF for sea creatures.

The world's LARGEST GUITAR-SHAPED BUILDING is Seminole Hard Rock Hotel and Casino in Hollywood, Florida.

WHITEHALL, the enormous Palm Beach mansion built in 1902 by hotel and railroad tycoon Henry Flagler, has 75 rooms! It's now a museum.

A hot tub for very large mermaids! MANATEES huddle together in the warm spillover water near the Florida Power and Light Company's Riviera Beach Plant.

Love lawn games? Try CROQUET. To play, you hit a ball with a long-handled mallet through wickets, or hoops. The National Croquet Center in West Palm Beach is the world's largest croquet facility.

Ride a WATER TAXI to explore Fort Lauderdale, known as the "Venice of America." The city has 300 miles of inland canals and waterways—just like Venice, Italy, does.

Gold Coast

It's time to shine! Break out your designer shades to catch some rays along the stylish "Gold Coast." How do you think the southeastern section of the state came by its nickname? Is it the glitzy stores and ritzy hotels in Palm Beach? The fast and flashy boats motoring the Intracoastal Waterway and Fort Lauderdale's canals? The golden sand beaches and sparkling sea? Or the gold coins spilling from wrecked pirate ships along Boca Raton's shoreline? Our vote: all of the above!

Palm Beach is one of the state's many BARRIER ISLANDS—a long, narrow island that's formed over time when sand piles onto a sandbar. Barrier islands run parallel to the mainland, protecting it from storms and high waves.

Plunge off one of the world's HIGHEST DIVE PLATFORMS (27 meters!) at the International Swimming Hall of Fame and Aquatic Center in Fort Lauderdale. It was designed to look like the hull of a ship.

Grammy-winning pop star ARIANA GRANDE grew up in Boca Raton. When she was eight years old, she performed on a cruise ship. Pop star Gloria Estefan was on board, heard Ariana, and told her to make singing her career!

Set sail to see over 1,300 yachts, sailing vessels, and motorboats at the Fort Lauderdale International Boat Show, the world's largest IN-WATER BOAT SHOW. It's no wonder Fort Lauderdale is called the "Yachting Capital of the World."

Even though Boca Raton means MOUTH OF THE RAT in Spanish, the city wasn't named for rodents. The words appeared on early sailing maps to show the location of hidden, sharp rocks that could gnaw at a ship's cables—just like a rat!

Food, Glorious Food

Florida food is delightfully delicious! You'll find the freshest catches from the sea, the juiciest citrus (oranges, grapefruit, tangerines), the spiciest Latin American fare, and the yummiest Caribbean snacks and sweets. Dig in!

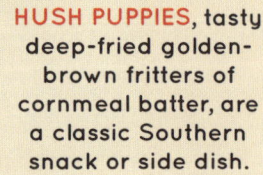

HUSH PUPPIES, tasty deep-fried golden-brown fritters of cornmeal batter, are a classic Southern snack or side dish.

KEY LIME PIE should be pale yellow and never, ever green! The official state pie is made from the juice of Key limes (named after the Florida Keys), which are the size of golf balls and have thinner rinds than other limes.

Stop at a citrus farm's roadside stand to gulp down a glass of **FRESH-SQUEEZED ORANGE JUICE,** the official state drink.

Bite into a warm, crispy **CUBANO SANDWICH,** made with roast pork, ham, Swiss cheese, mustard, and pickles pressed between thick Cuban bread. Popular in both Miami and Tampa, the Tampa version adds Genoa salami. Wash it down with a Jupiña pineapple soda.

Take a bite into a **PASTELITOS DE GUAYABA,** a warm, flaky pastry gushing with sweet guava and cream cheese.

STONE CRAB CLAWS are served cold with a tangy mustard dipping sauce. Fishers are only allowed to remove one claw per crab and then must set them free. These amazing crustaceans can regrow their claw!

If you like chicken tenders, you'll probably like **FRIED GATOR BITES**, made with alligator tail. It's a high-protein, low-fat meat.

BATIDO DE GUANÁBANA is a creamy milkshake made with soursop fruit, which tastes like banana with a citrus kick.

A meal in a package! **NACATAMALES** are the Nicaraguan version of tamales. Corn masa stuffed with meat, potatoes, rice, and veggies is wrapped and tied in a banana leaf.

Try **GRIYO**, or griot, a traditional Haitian dish of fried pork chunks served with a side of pikliz (pickled cabbage and vegetables).

Shrimply the best! **ROCK SHRIMP** taste like lobster! Found in deep water along the Gulf Coast and Titusville, their thick shells are hard as rocks.

The **PUB SUB**, or Publix chicken tender sub, is Florida famous! The Southern supermarket chain tucks breaded chicken tenders, cheese, and condiments into a doughy sub roll.

COCONUT PATTIES— creamy shredded coconut dipped in dark chocolate—are a Florida tradition.

PLANTAINS are cousins of bananas, but you can't eat them raw. Boil, bake, or fry them for a tasty treat!

More than 40 percent of Miami-Dade area residents were born in a foreign country. Many IMMIGRANTS came from Cuba, Venezuela, Nicaragua, Haiti, Colombia, Jamaica, and India.

Is that the clacking of DOMINO tiles? You're probably at Máximo Gómez Domino Park, or Domino Park, where older Cubans often spend the day playing the game and chatting with friends.

It's only SNOWED once in Miami—on January 19, 1977. And, as of 2023, the city has never had a recorded temperature in the single or triple digits.

Port of Miami is the world's BUSIEST CRUISE PORT.

Cool off with an icy RASPADO, or Nicaraguan snow cone, in Little Managua. The city of Sweetwater is home to the nation's largest population of Nicaraguan Americans and Nicaraguans.

Calle Ocho

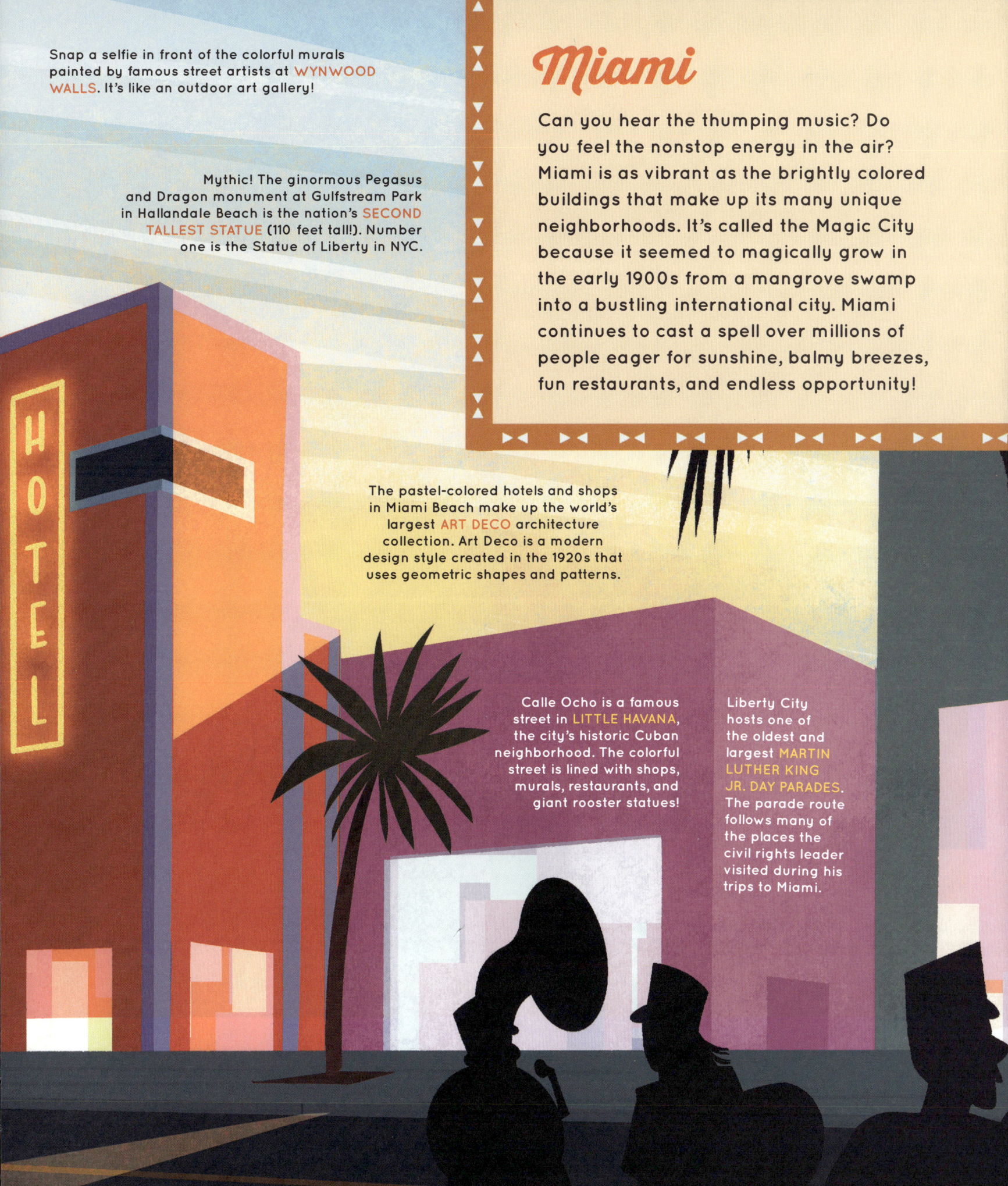

Snap a selfie in front of the colorful murals painted by famous street artists at WYNWOOD WALLS. It's like an outdoor art gallery!

Mythic! The ginormous Pegasus and Dragon monument at Gulfstream Park in Hallandale Beach is the nation's SECOND TALLEST STATUE (110 feet tall!). Number one is the Statue of Liberty in NYC.

Miami

Can you hear the thumping music? Do you feel the nonstop energy in the air? Miami is as vibrant as the brightly colored buildings that make up its many unique neighborhoods. It's called the Magic City because it seemed to magically grow in the early 1900s from a mangrove swamp into a bustling international city. Miami continues to cast a spell over millions of people eager for sunshine, balmy breezes, fun restaurants, and endless opportunity!

The pastel-colored hotels and shops in Miami Beach make up the world's largest ART DECO architecture collection. Art Deco is a modern design style created in the 1920s that uses geometric shapes and patterns.

HOTEL

Calle Ocho is a famous street in LITTLE HAVANA, the city's historic Cuban neighborhood. The colorful street is lined with shops, murals, restaurants, and giant rooster statues!

Liberty City hosts one of the oldest and largest MARTIN LUTHER KING JR. DAY PARADES. The parade route follows many of the places the civil rights leader visited during his trips to Miami.

Amazing Animals

Experience wildlife like nowhere else in the world! Because of its many diverse habitats, Florida has the most magnificent mix of unique animals. Let's go meet some!

ALLIGATORS swim and sun themselves throughout the state but AMERICAN CROCODILES, like the one below, only live in the southern tip. How do you tell them apart? Look at the snout. Alligators have wider, U-shaped snouts, and crocodiles have pointy, V-shaped snouts. Also a croc's bottom teeth can be seen when its mouth is closed, but a gator's lower teeth are hidden.

MANATEES, also called sea cows, are gentle giants that weigh close to 1,000 pounds! Since they're mammals they must rise for air, but they can hold their breath for up to 15 minutes! You can spot lots of manatees in Three Sisters Springs along Crystal River, the "Manatee Capital of the World."

The fierce FLORIDA PANTHER, the state animal, can leap up to 15 feet vertically when pouncing on prey but, unlike other mountain cats, is unable to roar. Only about 200 of the endangered wildcats are left in the wild, and they're protected at the Florida Panther National Wildlife Refuge in Immokalee.

Here's the scoop! The BROWN PELICAN uses the expandable pouch that dangles from its long bill as a fishing net. See the seabirds plunge-diving at the Pelican Island National Wildlife Refuge near Sebastian.

LOGGERHEAD TURTLES, named for their block-like head, build more than 60,000 nests on Florida's beaches. From May through October, Juno Beach is the densest sea turtle nesting ground in the world.

Spoiler alert: PALMETTO BUGS are actually Florida wood cockroaches. Their name probably came from the palmetto palm, where they like to hang out. Cockroaches are believed to be a whopping 300 million years old!

The MOCKINGBIRD can sing up to 200 different tunes and even mimic car alarms! It has been the state bird since 1927, but some residents say it should be replaced by a flamingo, wood stork, roseate spoonbill, Florida scrub jay, or an osprey. What do you say?

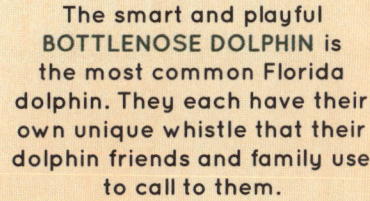

The smart and playful BOTTLENOSE DOLPHIN is the most common Florida dolphin. They each have their own unique whistle that their dolphin friends and family use to call to them.

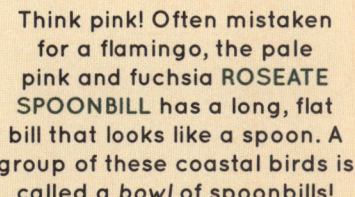

Think pink! Often mistaken for a flamingo, the pale pink and fuchsia ROSEATE SPOONBILL has a long, flat bill that looks like a spoon. A group of these coastal birds is called a *bowl* of spoonbills!

The white-tailed KEY DEER is about the size of a large dog and is the smallest North American deer. Found only in the Keys (mostly in Big Pine Key), they can swim between islands.

A tiny terror! Florida *hassssss* around 50 species of SNAKES, but only six are poisonous to humans. The very small, polka-dotted dusky pygmy rattlesnake is the state's most common venomous snake.

Hop to it! Found throughout Florida, the LITTLE GRASS FROG is the smallest frog in North America. These tiny frogs can jump 20 times their body length!

Guess how the ZEBRA LONGWING, the state butterfly, got its name! Its patterned wings warn predators: "Don't eat me—I'm toxic!"

Florida's WILD BOARS probably descended from a herd of pigs brought over by Spanish explorer Hernando de Soto in 1539. These huge hogs can weigh more than 300 pounds, or the same as a large refrigerator!

The Overseas Highway connects Florida's mainland to the Keys. There are 42 bridges and the longest is called SEVEN MILE BRIDGE. Can you guess its length? Nope, it's a trick. It's only 6.77 miles long!

Key West is the SOUTHERNMOST POINT of the continental U.S. (not including Hawaii, the southernmost state). Key West is only about 90 miles from Cuba, and it's on the same latitude line as Saudi Arabia and Egypt!

SPINY LOBSTERS—called "bugs"— don't have claws like their Maine cousins. After a storm or when it's migration time, they march single-file across the ocean floor, conga-style, to another location.

Is that a mermaid playing a "fluke-a-lele?" At THE LOWER KEYS UNDERWATER MUSIC FESTIVAL, divers and snorkelers in the waters of Looe Key Reef swim to a submerged soundtrack.

MIGRATING BIRDS, including peregrine falcons and 15 other species of raptors, usually make a pit stop in the Keys before continuing on to the Caribbean or Central and South America every fall.

Key West has the HIGHEST AVERAGE TEMPERATURE in the U.S.

In 2013, DIANA NYAD became the first person to swim from Cuba to Key West, Florida, without fins or a shark cage. It took her 53 hours!

Novelist JUDY BLUME, famous for her Fudge series, owns a bookstore in Key West!

Aquarius Reef Base, the world's only UNDERSEA RESEARCH LAB, is an algae-covered building that sits on the ocean floor off the coast of Key Largo.

The Keys

Splash! You'll find the perfect underwater playground in the Florida Keys. But these aren't the kind of keys used to open locks! "Key" comes from the Spanish word "cayo," meaning "small island." The Florida Keys are an archipelago, or a chain, of hundreds (maybe thousands—no one's counted) of tiny islands stretching far out into the ocean off of the state's southernmost tip. So slip on a pair of fins and a snorkel mask to *sea* North America's only living coral barrier reef for yourself!

Scuba diving is the only way to reach your room at the JULES' UNDERSEA LODGE in Key Largo. This completely underwater hotel sits 21 feet below the surface—the perfect spot for a squid to deliver room service!

Food fight! In 1982, after a U.S. Border Patrol checkpoint caused a huge traffic jam, the Keys declared it was seceding from, or leaving, the U.S. and would now be the CONCH REPUBLIC. Two minutes later, they surrendered—but not before tossing some conch fritters in protest!

The Ernest Hemingway Home and Museum is home to about 60 SIX-TOED CATS!

Only a few highly skilled Florida crabbers are allowed to harvest the treasured GOLDEN CRAB, found in waters as deep as 2,000 feet.

The WHITE SAND on Siesta Key beach stays cool to the touch even on the hottest day. Why? It's made up of 99 percent pure quartz crystal, which reflects light.

A CONCH is a giant sea snail that lives inside a spiral shell (the kind you can hear the ocean from when you put it to your ear). "Conchs" is also a nickname for people who live on the Keys.

Cool Inventions

Creative Floridians eagerly embrace the new, incredible, and never-before-seen. No idea is too wacky here! That's why the sunny state has given the world so many awesome inventions.

The first GLASS BOTTOM BOAT was invented in Silver Springs in 1878 by Hullam Jones and Philip Morrell. Jones added a glass viewing box to the bottom of a dugout canoe so tourists could peer into the clear waters.

Rolling in $$$! When Miami's in-line skaters in the mid 1990s didn't want to take off their skates to go into the bank, one bank installed the first ATM FOR IN-LINE SKATERS with a ramp to glide right up.

The assistant coach of the University of Florida Gators football team asked university scientists to help him find a way to keep his players hydrated in the heat. Led by James Robert Cade, they invented a drink to replace lost electrolytes and called it GATORADE. What's your favorite flavor?

Should you wear SUNSCREEN? The answer is "yes, yes, yes." Miami pharmacist Benjamin Green is credited with inventing sunscreen in 1944, to protect soldiers from the sun. Green sold his formula to Coppertone, making his the first sunscreen sold in the U.S.

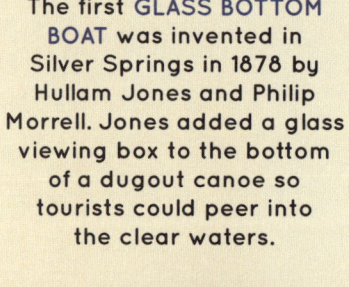

When socialite Lilly Pulitzer opened a juice stand in Palm Beach in 1959, she kept spilling orange juice on her white dresses. So she designed the colorful, patterned LILLY PULITZER DRESSES to hide the stains. Soon she was selling more dresses than juice!

The two Harris brothers from Miami borrowed money from their family and friends to open the first POLLO TROPICAL in 1988. The Caribbean-inspired fast-food chain now serves its famous citrus marinated chicken and fried yuca all over the Sunshine State.

After mechanic Bill France Sr. experienced cheating and a lack of rules at Daytona Beach's popular car race, he created the National Association for Stock Car Racing—or NASCAR, for short—in 1948 to organize the sport. The original cars looked very different from the ones we know today!

How do Floridians beat the steamy heat? Lots and lots of chilled air! You can thank Dr. John Gorrie of Apalachicola, whose early invention to cool hospital rooms in the 1840s led to the glorious wonder of AIR-CONDITIONING. He also invented the ICE-MAKING MACHINE. No wonder Apalachicola has a museum celebrating this cool dude.

VENTANITAS, walk-up windows where you can order pastelitos, croquetas, and coffee, were created by Felipe Valls Sr., who owned Versailles Restaurant in Miami. His sliding window let customers be served while keeping the air-conditioning from escaping.

Insta-Burger King was the name of the fast-food restaurant in Jacksonville that Keith Kramer and Matthew Burns opened in 1953. A few years later, when James McLamore and David Edgerton bought the company, they renamed it BURGER KING and created their famous Whopper. It was cooked on an open-flame broiler (a big deal back then) and cost 29 cents.

When George Jenkins opened PUBLIX in the 1940s in Winter Haven, it was one of the first food stores with air-conditioning, automatic doors, and fluorescent lighting. Fun fact: kids get a free cookie at the Publix bakery— just ask (politely)!

Upset that local hospitals refused to help Black patients, Tampa nurse Clara C. Frye created a HOSPITAL INSIDE HER HOME in 1908. Her dining room table was the operating table. She later built the first hospital in Tampa that didn't discriminate or make people pay if they couldn't afford it. The hospital ran for 28 years.

Play dirty! In 1921, Ed Frank from Bonita Springs invented what's now known as the SWAMP BUGGY. Balloon-like tires helped hunters drive through murky bogs and muddy swamps. The first official World Famous Swamp Buggy Race was held in Naples in 1949, and buggies still compete on the Mile O' Mud track.

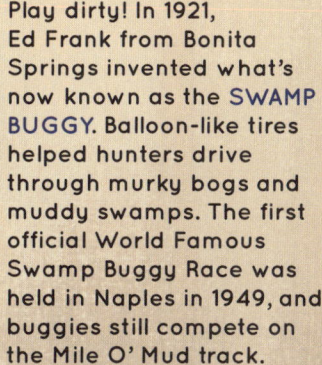

FROZEN ORANGE JUICE CONCENTRATE was created so soldiers during World War II could get vitamin C. Fresh orange juice spoiled, so scientists invented a way to remove the extra liquid, then freeze it to ship overseas. When the concentrate is plopped into a pitcher of water and stirred, it becomes juice again! This invention made the Florida orange business boom.

Everglades National Park

Teeming with thick saw grass, duckweed, cypress, mangroves, and wildlife galore, Everglades National Park takes up much of the state's southern tip. Here's a question: is the Everglades a swamp? No! It's a slow-moving, very shallow, very wide river. It's not a true swamp because it has water that's constantly moving. In fact, the Glades' nickname is "River of Grass." Let's hop into an airboat to experience an incredible ecosystem that's unlike anything anywhere else in the world.

What's the state's most vicious animal? The MOSQUITO! During the wet summer season, bloodthirsty "skeeters" buzz supreme. As annoying as they may be, mosquitoes are a vital part of the Glades' food chain.

Pee-ew! Is a SKUNK APE lurking about? The legendary Bigfoot-like beast believed to roam the Everglades is said to be giant, hairy, and very, very stinky.

Flat-bottom AIRBOATS zoom across the top of the shallow water. They're also called fanboats because the huge fan on the back acts like a propeller.

The Glades is the only place in the world where BOTH ALLIGATORS AND CROCODILES live together in the wild. Crocs mostly stick to the coastal saltwater areas, while gators stay inland near freshwater.

Leaf me alone! The MANCHINEEL is one of the world's most dangerous trees. A bite of its green apple-like fruit or a drop of its sap on your skin causes painful blisters and even death! It's thought the Calusa warrior's arrow that killed Ponce de León was dipped in Manchineel sap.

Florida has the largest population of BALD EAGLES in the lower 48 states.

Everglades National Park is the THIRD LARGEST NATIONAL PARK in the contiguous U.S., behind Yellowstone and Death Valley. It's bigger than the state of Delaware! The wetlands used to cover 4,000 square miles. But with all the construction and drainage, only half of that remains today.

The AH-TAH-THI-KI MUSEUM celebrates the history and traditions of the unconquered Seminole people, past and present. "Ah-Tah-Thi-Ki" means "a place to learn, a place to remember."

The enormous BURMESE PYTHON threatens the ecosystem by eating whatever fits into its mouth, including an entire alligator *whole*—while still alive! These invasive snakes were probably introduced when someone foolishly released their pets in the Glades.

Everglades National Park has North America's largest MANGROVE forest. Mangroves, a cluster of trees that can grow in salty environments, help keep the water clean and shelter sea creatures.

The PIG FROG's croak sounds like a pig's grunt. They eat insects, crayfish—and sometimes each other! Because their skin easily absorbs liquids, scientists study them to see if there are toxins in the wetlands.

Spooky! The GHOST ORCHID is one of the rarest flowers in the world. It has a delicate pale bloom and roots that wrap around a tree's trunk. Only the giant sphinx moth can pollinate it.

Water from LAKE OKEECHOBEE, the state's largest freshwater lake, empties into the Everglades. The Everglades provides drinking water for one out of every three Floridians. That's one of the reasons the health of the fragile Glades is a big deal.

Fun Festivals

The spirit of Florida is loud and proud at festivals that are a bit offbeat! From frog legs to conga lines and wiggling worms, there's something for everyone. Let the celebrations begin!

Dish up some possum ice cream at the WAUSAU POSSUM FESTIVAL. It's made out of the fruit persimmons, not possum. It seems possums are partial to persimmons!

Squeeze the day, kumquat may! Try tangy kumquat pie and marmalade at the KUMQUAT FESTIVAL in Dade City. The nearby town of St. Joseph is known as the "Kumquat Capital of the World." Fun fact: kumquats are the only citrus fruit you can eat whole—skin and all.

Hop over to Fellsmere's FROG LEG FESTIVAL, which holds the record for the most frog legs served in one day.

Berry yummy! More than 200,000 STRAWBERRY SHORTCAKES TOPPED WITH WHIPPED CREAM, the official state dessert, are served during the Florida Strawberry Festival in Plant City.

Enter the watermelon seed-spitting contest at the Chiefland WATERMELON FESTIVAL. Watermelon contains 92 percent water, so it's no mystery how this juicy fruit got its name.

The SEBRING SODA FESTIVAL is Florida's fizziest festival! Sample over 200 different sodas from around the world, including Key lime cream, butterscotch root beer, and alien snot!

Buzz to the TUPELO HONEY FESTIVAL under the great mossy oaks of Lake Alice in Wewahitchka. White tupelo trees in the Apalachicola River Valley only bloom in April and May, so busy bees must collect the sweet nectar that produces this rare honey quickly.

Z is for zucchini! Celebrate the spectacular squash at the WINDSOR ZUCCHINI FESTIVAL with zucchini ice cream and a contest for the biggest, ugliest, and best-carved zucchinis.

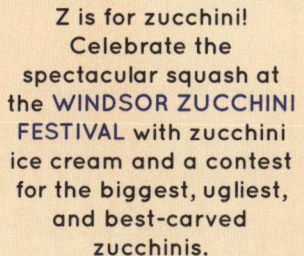

At the SOPCHOPPY WORM GRUNTIN' FESTIVAL, contestants rub wooden sticks and metal together to charm earthworms aboveground. The vibrations trick the worms into thinking a mole is after them, so they squirm up to get away, only to be captured for fishing bait.

Step on the art! Sarasota gets covered with spectacular 3D pavement paintings at the CHALK FESTIVAL. You could start your own chalk festival on the sidewalk by your home or school!

Celebrate the crustaceans living in the salt marshes and mud at Steinhatchee's FIDDLER CRAB FESTIVAL. Fun fact: male fiddler crabs have one giant claw that looks (kind of) like a violin.

Cha-cha-cha! The world record for the longest CONGA LINE—119,986 dancers!—was set in 1988 at the Calle Ocho Music Festival in Miami's Little Havana neighborhood. With over a million visitors each year, it's the country's largest Hispanic celebration.

Let 'em fly! At the FLORA-BAMA INTERSTATE MULLET TOSS in Perdido Key, contestants toss dead mullets (a Florida fish) as far as they can across the state line into Alabama.

Paradise Coast

Don't worry, *beach* happy! Along the "Paradise Coast" on the southwestern side of the state, dolphin pods play, fishing boats bob, and sea creatures swim in the calm, sparkling-blue Gulf of Mexico waters. And wait until you see the big and beautiful seashells piled high on the beaches! You can scoop them up by the handful. *Shell* we stop and have a *shellabration*?

There are BONNETS AND BICYCLES (and no cell phones) in Pinecraft, a winter vacation spot for sun-seeking Amish and Mennonite peoples.

The WORLD'S LARGEST MINIATURE CIRCUS at the Ringling Circus Museum in Sarasota has 42,000 tiny pieces and took 50 years to construct. Sarasota was once the winter home of the famous Ringling Bros and Barnum and Bailey circus.

BAILEY-MATTHEWS NATIONAL SHELL MUSEUM in Sanibel is the only museum in the country that's all about shells and mollusks (the creatures who make the shells). The study of mollusks is called malacology, and the study of the exoskeleton or hard shell is called conchology.

The HORSE CONCH, the state shell, is the largest living snail in North America. It captures its prey with its brilliant orange-red foot. Native people once used the shells as tools and drinking cups.

Called the "Shark Lady," ichthyologist (a scientist who studies fish) DR. EUGENIE CLARK once rode on the back of a 50-foot whale shark! (Never try this yourself!) She founded the Mote Marine Laboratory in Sarasota for shark and marine mammal research.

Canoeing down the Peace River is a great spot for FOSSIL HUNTING!

Whoever named TEN THOUSAND ISLANDS, a maze of mangrove islands near Marco Island, sure liked to exaggerate. No one has an exact count, but it's probably more like a few hundred uninhabited small islands.

At low tide, search for the rare JUNONIA, LION'S PAW, SCOTCH BONNET, or ALPHABET CONE shells. If you find a junonia, the local newspapers may publish your photo! But remember to put any shell with a living animal inside back in the water.

The AMERICAN SAND SCULPTING CHAMPIONSHIPS on Fort Myers Beach is like the Olympics of sandcastle building.

Venice is called the "Shark Tooth Capital of the World." Dig in the sand to uncover ANCIENT SHARK TEETH that have washed ashore. The best times to search are early morning or right after a storm.

Prawn to be wild! How many pounds of PINK SHRIMP can you eat in eight minutes? Find out at the annual Fort Myers Beach Shrimp Festival's shrimp eating contest. Their shell color comes from the pink coral sand they digest.

TYPES OF SHELLS

Change Makers

Countless creative and courageous Floridians have transformed our world. We chose just a handful of the many influential pioneers, recording artists, authors, activists, athletes, and leaders to feature. Many were the first from their community to achieve a goal, effect change, or do something super cool.

Superstar author ZORA NEALE HURSTON (1891–1960) grew up in Eatonville, the nation's first self-governing all-Black town. After becoming the first Black graduate from Barnard College, NYC, she introduced the world to the racial struggles of the rural South. *Their Eyes Were Watching God* is her best-known book. Celebrate her life at the ZORA! Festival in Eatonville.

Known to many as "Her Deepness," marine biologist DR. SYLVIA EARLE (1935–) has led more than a hundred marine expeditions (with over 7,000 hours of scuba diving!) and was the first woman named chief scientist at the National Oceanic and Atmospheric Administration. She first discovered the ocean upon moving to Dunedin at age 12 and encourages all kids to swim in its glorious waters so they'll understand why it needs protecting.

"Be a nuisance where it counts," environmental champion MARJORY STONEMAN DOUGLAS (1890–1998) once said. Called "Mother of the Everglades," she never stopped showing how vital conservation is. Her book, *The Everglades: River of Grass*, exposed threats from building roads, and she helped defeat a plan to build an airport in the Everglades.

In 1953, COLONEL JACQUELINE "JACKIE" COCHRAN (1910–1980) became the first woman to fly faster than the speed of sound. Growing up in the Panhandle, she worked in cotton mills at age eight. She learned to fly airplanes in her twenties. During World War II, she became the first woman to ferry a bomber plane overseas and trained hundreds of other women pilots. She holds the most speed, altitude, and distance records of *any* pilot!

The only woman to have founded a major U.S. city, JULIA TUTTLE (1849–1898) is called the "Mother of Miami." In the 1890s, the land she owned north of the Miami River was thick swamp. Tuttle persuaded tycoon Henry Flagler to extend his railroad from West Palm Beach to the Biscayne Bay. In 1896, the city of Miami was formed. Tuttle opened the city's first bakery, dairy, and was a director of the bank.

After leaving his family in China for the U.S. as a teenager, LUE GIM GONG (1860–1925) eventually worked in the orange groves of DeLand, Florida. Everyone quickly realized he had a green thumb! He combined different orange varieties and produced fruit that could better survive winter freezes and would ripen later. This let Florida's growers ship fruit north throughout the year.

The great Seminole warrior OSCEOLA (1804–1838) was born in present-day Alabama but forced to live in Spanish Florida. In 1835, when the U.S. government tried to take Seminole land and push his people onto a reservation, he and a group of warriors fought back, sparking the Second Seminole War. The army arranged for peace talks, but it was a trap. Osceola was captured and died in prison.

Micanopy resident ARCHIE CARR (1909–1987) was a world-famous reptile scientist at the University of Florida. Called the "Father of Sea Turtle Research," he was the first to warn that the sea turtles were in danger and needed protecting. His birthday (June 16) is International Sea Turtle Day, and the Archie Carr National Wildlife Refuge in Melbourne Beach is an important nesting area for loggerhead sea turtles.

Pop music icon and seven-time Grammy winner GLORIA ESTEFAN (1957–) put Latin music on the pop charts. Her family moved to Miami after the Cuban Revolution. When she was 18, Emilio Estefan invited her to be the lead singer of his band, later renamed the Miami Sound Machine. They introduced Latin beats and Cuban sounds into mainstream American music with hits such as "Conga" and "Rhythm Is Gonna Get You."

Tennis legend CHRIS EVERT (1954–) was the first player, male or female, to win 1,000 singles matches. She grew up in Fort Lauderdale, practicing every day with her father. Because she was so small, she developed her trademark powerful two-handed backhand. She was ranked either No. 1 or No. 2 in the world from 1975 to 1986. She helped women's tennis soar in popularity.

There's no time like prime time! Football and baseball player DEION SANDERS (1967–) is the only athlete to play in both a Super Bowl and a World Series. He's also the only player to score an NFL touchdown and hit an MLB home run in the same week! His nickname "Prime Time" started while playing high school basketball in Fort Myers. He then played football, baseball, and ran track at Florida State University.

Educator and racial and gender equality champion DR. MARY MCLEOD BETHUNE (1875–1955) is known as the "First Lady of the Struggle" because she worked so hard to better Black American lives. In 1904, she opened a school for Black girls with just five students and $1.50. It became Bethune-Cookman University. She advised five U.S. presidents and was the first Black American with a statue in the National Statuary Hall Collection at the U.S. Capitol.

Sun Coast

You always bring your own sunshine wherever you go, so we know you'll be radiating extra awesomeness on the "Sun Coast!" The west-central coastline boasts the most solar rays in the state. Slather on the sunscreen and hop on your bicycle 'cause we're joining the stream of runners, skateboarders, and dog walkers that fill Tampa and St. Petersburg's many waterfront pathways. You'll need plenty of pedal power—at 4.5 miles, Tampa's Bayshore Boulevard is the nation's longest sidewalk! As you round the curves, keep an eye out for frolicking bottlenose dolphins and an ear open for laughing gulls (their call sounds like a high-pitched laugh) in and above Tampa Bay. What a perfect sunny-side-up day!

Want to visit a foreign country and be back in the U.S. before lunch? Step into JOSÉ MARTÍ PARK in Ybor City, and you'll literally be standing on Cuban soil. The small park belongs to Cuba and is protected by an international treaty.

"THE BIG GUAVA," Tampa's nickname, started from a rumor in the 1800s that tons of wild guava trees grew here. They didn't, but people showed up to look for them anyway.

La Segunda Bakery in Ybor City is the world's largest producer of CUBAN BREAD. They bake 18,000 crusty loaves each day.

The SUNSHINE SKYWAY BRIDGE over Tampa Bay is one of the largest cable-stayed concrete bridges in North America. It reaches 4.1 miles across and soars 190 feet above the water!

The name TAMPA comes from the Calusa language and means "sticks of fire." Maybe it's because Tampa experiences so much lightning!

The Lagoon at Epperson in Wesley Chapel is the nation's LARGEST SWIMMING POOL (328,739 sq ft).

St. Petersburg holds the world record for the most days of SUNSHINE in a row—768!

Tarpon Springs calls itself the "SPONGE CAPITAL OF THE WORLD," supplying roughly 70 percent of the world's natural sea sponges. In the early 1900s, divers from the Greek islands settled here to harvest Gulf sponges, and today the town has the most Greek American residents in the nation.

TAMPA BAY is incredibly shallow (only about 12 feet deep on average), so artificial channels had to be dredged to let ships sail in. It's Florida's largest open-water estuary.

ST. PETERSBURG, also called "St. Pete," was almost named Detroit. The story goes that two men purchased the land together, and each wanted to name it after his hometown (St. Petersburg in Russia and Detroit in Michigan). So they flipped a coin. Guess who won!

A chicken crossed the road in Ybor City . . . and that's no joke! The WILD CHICKENS that strut the city's streets and parks are descendants of the flocks that Cuban immigrants brought to Florida over 100 years ago.

Madeira Beach calls itself the "Grouper Capital of the World." Fun fact: the GOLIATH GROUPER can weigh 800 pounds and measure more than 8 feet in length!

Join swashbuckling kids in eye patches at the CHILDREN'S GASPARILLA PIRATE FEST in Tampa.

Farmers love Tampa! The city's number one export is PHOSPHATE, a mineral used to create fertilizers.

¡Wepa! COLUMBIA RESTAURANT in Ybor City has 15 dining rooms and 1,700 seats! It is the oldest Spanish restaurant in the U.S. and the largest Spanish restaurant in the world.

The Awe of Mother Nature

Hurricanes and lightning and sinkholes—oh my! Mother Nature likes to go wild—and wet—in the Sunshine State. But no matter what natural hazard is thrown their way, Floridians know the secret to staying safe: being prepared. They gather supplies, create plans, evacuate if needed, watch where they walk, and always keep an eye on the sky.

It's a Wild Wildlife

Leapin' lizards! FROZEN IGUANAS are falling from the sky! When temps drop in South Florida, the green reptiles' bodies shut down and they go tumbling out of the trees. Don't worry, they're not dead. Just temporarily inactive.

Let's Hear It for Limestone

Florida has the MOST UNDERWATER SPRINGS in the world (700!) because the limestone rock beneath your feet is soft with many holes, like Swiss cheese, so rain soaks into it. Springs are openings in the rock that let the warm water flow and bubble out. WAKULLA SPRINGS is one of the nation's largest and deepest freshwater springs.

Wakulla County has the nation's LARGEST UNDERWATER CAVE SYSTEM. The caves are actually really big holes in the limestone!

When hurricanes hit, Florida's zoos and botanical gardens often shelter their FLAMINGOS in the public bathrooms.

A Hole in One

Limestone is also the reason why Florida has the most SINKHOLES in the country. When too much water collects or if too many buildings or roads are built, fragile limestone can weaken and collapse into a sinkhole—sometimes pulling roads and houses down with it!

The massive bowl-shaped sinkhole with a blue pond at the bottom of DEVIL'S MILLHOPPER GEOLOGICAL STATE PARK in Gainesville is over 10,000 years old.

Falling Waters State Park is home to Florida's tallest WATERFALL. How tall? No one knows, because it falls directly into a fern-covered sinkhole.

Flash and Boom

The area from Tampa Bay to Titusville is called LIGHTNING ALLEY because it experiences the most lightning strikes in the country. When you see a flash of lightning, count the number of seconds until you hear the boom of thunder. Divide that number by five and that's how many miles away the lightning is from you.

Blowin' in the Wind

Kids in other states get school snow days, but Florida students get HURRICANE DAYS. About 40 percent of the world's hurricanes slam the Sunshine State. A tropical storm turns into a hurricane once winds gust over 74 miles per hour (mph).

HURRICANES HAVE NAMES. The first one of the year is given a name beginning with the letter A. Letters Q, U, X, Y, and Z are skipped. Six different name lists alternate each year, but if a hurricane causes major damage, its name is retired and replaced with another.

The SAFFIR-SIMPSON HURRICANE WIND SCALE was developed by two Floridians (of course!). It ranks hurricanes from Category 1 (winds between 74 and 95 mph) to Category 5 (winds over 157 mph), so you know the power of the storm heading your way.

Some of the strongest hurricanes to hit Florida:
• The Category 5 Labor Day Hurricane of 1935 struck the Keys with winds around 180 mph.
• Hurricane Andrew, a Category 5, slammed into southern Miami-Dade County in 1992 with winds of 165 mph.
• Hurricane Michael blasted the Panhandle in 2018 with winds around 160 mph, making it a Category 5.
• Category 4 Hurricane Ian devastated the Gulf Coast in 2022 with winds around 150 mph.

Twisted and crooked palm trees that had survived Hurricane Andrew's intense winds were used to design SEUSS LANDING at Universal's Islands of Adventure in Orlando.

Before the invention of weather satellites, Grady Norton overheard mourners at a funeral in 1928 wish there'd been a way to warn the people who had died in a big hurricane. From then on, Norton devoted his life to tracking hurricanes and saving lives. He became the director of the first NATIONAL HURRICANE CENTER, which is now in Miami.

Emerald Coast

There's a saying in Florida, "The farther north you go, the more south it gets." Get ready for heaps of Southern charm and hospitality, because we're rolling into Northwest Florida, known as the "Panhandle" or "Emerald Coast." Any guesses where these nicknames came from? Ooh, you're smart! The region *is* shaped like the handle of a frying pan, and the clear, warm Gulf waters glow a beautiful emerald green. The Panhandle is famous for miles of sugary-white sand beaches, enchanted natural springs, parks filled with Spanish moss–draped trees, the state capital, *and* the most epic sunsets ever.

The "Mighty O" and "Great Carrier Reef" are nicknames for sunken former aircraft carrier USS *Oriskany*, which sits 212 feet under Pensacola Bay. It's the world's LARGEST ARTIFICIAL REEF.

How strong is your sandcastle game? You can hire a SANDCASTLE COACH for tips on creating a sand-tastic masterpiece.

The Appalachian Mountains that run along the country's East Coast and Florida's Apalachicola River get credit for the incredibly soft, white sand beaches. Over 20,000 years ago, QUARTZ from the mountains eroded and the crystal particles washed down the river, piling up as sand along the coast.

Time flies in Beacon Hill! It's one of the few towns in the U.S. that shares TWO DIFFERENT TIME ZONES. So the house across the street could be an hour ahead or behind you! The Apalachicola River divides Eastern Standard Time (called "fast time" here) and Central Standard Time ("slow time").

Apalachicola Bay is famous for producing some of the country's biggest and best OYSTERS.

Pensacola Bay is home to the U.S. Navy and U.S. Marine Corps's BLUE ANGELS, one of the world's most elite flying teams. In some of their high-speed maneuvers, planes flying 700 miles per hour cross just 18 inches apart (the width of most toilet seats!).

It's easy to reel in saltwater fish in Destin, often called the WORLD'S LUCKIEST FISHING VILLAGE.

The world's LARGEST AMERICAN FLAG MURAL is in Destin and was painted by Robert Wyland.

Golden-yellow SEA OATS sway in the Gulf breeze. Their deep, sturdy roots anchor the sand dunes in place during storms and hurricanes. That's why it's against the law to pick them.

One of the main reasons Tallahassee was picked to be STATE CAPITAL in 1824 was its location—halfway between the port cities of Pensacola and St. Augustine.

On a beach near Tallahassee in 2023, a family discovered a huge clam that scientists estimated to be 214 years old. (They found its age by counting the layers on its shell.) Named "Aber-clam Lincoln" because it was born the same year as the former president, the OLD CLAM was released back into the ocean.

Sea creatures jostle with scuba divers to get a front-row view of the sculptures at the UNDERWATER MUSEUM OF ART, off the coast of Grayton Beach State Park and 58 feet down.

Are we there yet? The marshes of St. Marks National Wildlife Refuge are one of the last snack stops for millions of migrating MONARCH BUTTERFLIES before they fly over the Gulf to Mexico.

Weird, Weirder, Weirdest

It's no secret that Florida can be super quirky when it wants to be, and sometimes fabulous stuff doesn't neatly fit into any one category. But that's kind of the definition of quirky, right? So we've gathered up the extra oddness for you right here!

Twistee Treat sells soft serve from **ICE-CREAM-CONE-SHAPED BUILDINGS.**

Florida is the only state with an **EMBASSY** in Washington, D.C. Its mission is to champion Florida to the world, so, of course, all visitors get a glass of fresh-squeezed OJ!

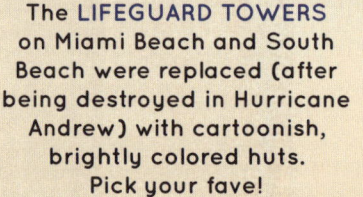

George Frandsen of Bradenton set a Guinness World Record for the largest collection of **FOSSILIZED POOP,** known as coprolites. But they didn't come from Florida because the state was underwater when dinosaurs were alive, so none roamed, or pooped, here.

The **LIFEGUARD TOWERS** on Miami Beach and South Beach were replaced (after being destroyed in Hurricane Andrew) with cartoonish, brightly colored huts. Pick your fave!

Ho, ho, hang ten! Every Christmas Eve, hundreds of **SURFING SANTAS** ride the waves in Cocoa Beach.

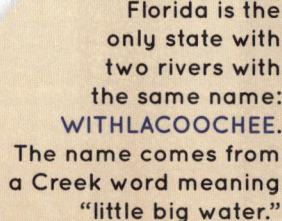

Florida is the only state with two rivers with the same name: **WITHLACOOCHEE.** The name comes from a Creek word meaning "little big water."

Cars appear to ROLL UPHILL at Spook Hill in Lake Wales! Is it an optical illusion or something else?

The WORLD'S SMALLEST POLICE STATION is in an old phone booth in Carrabelle!

Florida's cowboys were once called COW HUNTERS, because cattle roundups in the dense swamp, scrub, and forests were like games of hide-and-seek! The first cow hunters hailed from the Seminole Nation.

The WORLD'S SMALLEST POST OFFICE was a toolshed before becoming a post office in Ochopee!

MagLab (National High Magnetic Field Laboratory) in Tallahassee is the largest and highest-powered MAGNET LAB in the world. Some of their magnets are more than a million times stronger than the Earth's magnetic field!

Psst, here's the dirt . . . Florida has an official soil! MYAKKA FINE SAND is only found in Florida. It allows the state to grow so many yummy crops.

About 250 TOILET SEATS commemorating birthdays, weddings, and family vacations decorate a channel, or cut, on the bayside of Plantation Key.

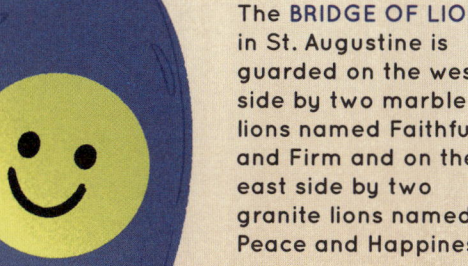

The BRIDGE OF LIONS in St. Augustine is guarded on the west side by two marble lions named Faithful and Firm and on the east side by two granite lions named Peace and Happiness.

For over seven decades, mystical MERMAIDS have been swimming—and performing—at Weeki Wachee Springs State Park!

Spider monkeys swing from tree to tree on their own private MONKEY ISLAND in the middle of the Homosassa River. They're descendants of monkeys used to research the polio vaccine. Because they were quite mischievous—climbing into tourists' cars and stealing candy—the monkeys were given a safe space all to themselves.

Index

Major League Professional Sports Teams

National Football League
Jacksonville Jaguars, Miami Dolphins,
Tampa Bay Buccaneers

Major League Baseball
Miami Marlins, Tampa Bay Rays

National Basketball Association
Miami Heat, Orlando Magic

Major League Soccer
Inter Miami CF, Orlando City SC

National Women's Soccer League
Orlando Pride

National Hockey League
Florida Panthers, Tampa Bay Lightning